isbn 978-0-578-00847-9

8slices

writings from 2006-2008

todd richmond

toc

preface

These writings were originally posted on my blog over a three year period during and post-divorce. One might think that at 45 years of age one would have things relatively under control, but that myth was quickly trounced. Yet out of chaos can come enlightenment or at least bemusement. Either way, the creative process was fueled and took off in a variety of directions. Poetry on my blog, photos on the internets and elsewhere, live music performed solo and in groups, and youtube videos of an alter ego, harkening back to decades before.

The utmost respect, sincere thanks, and deepest love for those that crossed my path during those three years and beyond. This is about all of it, through my filter, and with my somewhat twisted take on the language.

If you can see some of yourself or your life in any of this that is great, but realize that things are not always as they seem, especially in my creative output. There...that sounds like a fine disclaimer.

Thanks to my son, Calvin, for showing me the depth of creativity and odds ways in which things get reified. Thanks to st for patience and critical analysis as well as participation in the process. And thanks to those who have crossed my path and likely don't realize how much they touched me. Namaste.

first slice

early 2006

edge dance

the magic is found on the edge
the ragged edge
make it dance
not step and fetch
always pushing until I let it go
let it flow
empty mind that I can find
but notice and it's gone

you can't chase it
you can't erase it
you can't base it
on where you've been before

it means so much
to let it go
seek it you will not find
a voice standing
imagination landing
on top of it all

sometimes

sometimes you get a good night's sleep
sometimes you don't
sometimes your dreams are ok
sometimes they're not (but always interesting)
sometimes you think you're doing ok
sometimes you don't
sometimes your body hurts
sometimes it doesn't
sometimes you say the right thing
sometimes you don't
sometimes your words make someone smile
sometimes they don't
sometimes you think it matters
sometimes it doesn't
sometimes you're able to be in the moment
sometimes you're not
sometimes you think it was you
sometimes it wasn't

sometime is always now
except when it isn't

rooftop

your heart pulls at me just like an entertainer
yeah, but you're up a little too high
ain't no thing but tell me please what's the truth
i feel like you left it all out to die

up there on the rooftop
you said this was strong
shine a light, shine all day

your friends know I would be like some intruder
could have been the one that stole your heart
you had to say our time alone was golden
how was I to know, another by your side

so why then are you singing
that I could be your king?
i never need it, I don't believe it

it hurt me so to lose you, I hand it right to me
ain't got much to say, someone else to blame
ain't got much to say, so long

you say love the sinner, have them to dinner
then when I try you won't take my call
i just take to suffering in silence
i'll never figure out your heart

thought you pulled a fast one, but I try to learn
story of my life, a story for my daughter

up there on the rooftop
you said that kiss was wrong
ain't got much to say, someone else to blame
ain't got much to say, so long

it hurt me so to lose you, I hand it right to me
shine a light, shine on me

up there on the rooftop
you told me this was strong
ain't got much to say, someone else to blame

sniuppet

how do you take it as it comes
how do you learn to walk, not run
a world that turns so fast
makes today feel like the past

lyric turn

while I contemplate my sad behavior
I sit and drink it in quiet displeasure
those cruel shoes laugh and giggle
and remind me that the journey is stained

nothing

you enter with nothing
you leave with nothing
all you have is the journey
and what you find along the way

mercy street

Grace's fraternal twin sister, Mercy visits me from time to time. Sometimes Peter has to hit me over the head to acknowledge it. And sometimes Mercy isn't sweet and supportive, but instead sad and rips and tears. Not because she means to cause pain, quite the contrary. But the cold hard reality is that to be able to greet Mercy, the scars have to be pierced. And that hurts. I remember being on my knees, looking for Mercy. She was there, looking over my shoulder. But unable to speak. I turned, seeing double from the tears and the fear. Mercy and Grace a fleeting vision as they looked at each other and walked. Unable to help except in my dreams. Until I could wear my inside out.

I press the string and a note sings. It's sweet, then it fades, only to be replaced by another as the key shifts. They move into the void in a vain attempt to fill it. The lesson that has to be learned again and again. There's tenderness in the void. The empty space between the notes. Trying to fill it chases the love and joy away. Let it sit. Damp the string and pause. Sit out a beat. Then ease in gently. There is a time to slap. And a time to let it bloom. And a time to sit out. Not quitting. There is a reason they call them rests. Another bar will come around. It always does. Until it doesn't. Then you're done. Try not to think about it, Alice. Say hello to Grace and Mercy.

Is this what I'm supposed to be doing? I guess we'll find out. Because if I don't at least ask the question, then I'll never know. And there are some things that you need to know. Or at least ask. Live the question...

tired of it all

twist and stretch
and try to pull
yourself out of the car
or out of the bed
or out of a rut
same old patterns
but a different time
and place and space

can't go on the side
or bend to flex
holding fluid
won't go down
you hold it up
and tuck your arm
and hope your weight
doesn't pull her down
or pull you down

but you'll fall down
because what goes up
must come down
and sometimes further
down than you think
you can't feel or see

so you didn't
but now you do
because you can
doesn't make it easy
doesn't make it right
does make me tired
of it all

last time seen

a cut up, a card
kissing the darkness
embracing a doorway
in a dream not blessed
with a street named mercy

driven the loop
a faded dash
warped from the heat
and years that passed
a decade down

you never know
the last time scene
and sand between
walk up the stairs
last time seen

second slice

late 2006

the idea guy

be careful what you wish for is what they say
the Chinese say, "may you live in interesting times."
i'm Chinese don't you know
even though a cold wind blows

my wheels turn 24/7 but that's what they want
they pay you for those cycles and gears
i'm quite tired don't you know
and on the TV nothing but snow

the idea guy walks at a pace
that scares you if you bother to notice
he thinks to keep the demons down
but they won't leave his town

he's smart and manic and bursting forth
he can be quite a handful sources say
afraid of making another one of himself
letting her walk he climbs on the shelf

it turns out that outliers are lonely
when the mania fades into sackcloth
it's been years since he got ashes
and around the corner another crashes

the idea guy runs until empty
but find the reserve and starts over again
he fights to keep the demons down
anything to avoid a backless gown

devil mind middle round

deja vu all over again
fighting it
in measured doses
and an attempt to be
someone I'm not
or someone I am
or at this point just be
devil mind spins on its axis
throwing muses that cannot help
gouging a hole in the table
that i'll have to fix

I've fixed holes where the rain gets in
to try and stop my mind from wandering
where it will go
where it can go
where it must go
driven by dark shadows and
steel glances from the time of 8

step up and get it right
step up and take what you're owed
step up and take a man
bring dishonor to ourselves and family
we live through you, you bastard
get it fucking right.

but what if I don't? what if I can't?
What if the point is to get it wrong. So very wrong.
And show the others how not to do it.
Is there not value in my failure?
It may be ugly and difficult.
But there is beauty and elegance in the difficulty.

Difficulty hovers like a hawk,
circling empowerment
empowerment puts on a good show
but really doesn't know as she is depending on
the hawk to tell her what to think
and what to breath
and when to die

It is not now. It is not tomorrow.
It is when the muse releases
us to create the note and world
and find a spot to carry out
some work in peace
some work in love
some work in joy.

shine on

a crazy pearl you travel the world
and often change shape
they're your means of escape

shine on, shine on
brighter than the heavens
shine on, shine on

climb into one mind
for fear you won't find
the baby within
but she's there,
she's beautiful, she's there

shine on, shine on
the universe is smiling
shine on, shine on

your brilliance so bright
you seem to lose sight
of the power inside
and the love that you ride

like a dragon with a pearl
you'll turn around the world
and take the shaky steps
realize the promises kept

shine on, shine on
your power is growing
shine on, shine on
your beauty is showing
shine on, shine on
the muses are throwing
a party for you

love always, love well
shine always, shine well
shine on, shine on

cleaned up

everybody is moving on
got their mojo working
kissing the sky
with the pains tucked away
and good riddance to the hurt

rocking like a baby
the runners always give their feel
from one ordeal
to another, the river bends
and fades around and tends
to the carriage car

knowing less than before
makes me sit uneasy
and a bit queasy
from that second drink
there's a minimum
you angry chrysanthemum

every night changes hue
shapes and lines block
take stock, lightly mock
a wagging finger, strapping dagger
plunged into worry

it bleeds dark hues
i said it changed the night
alters sight, you said it would be alright
but it isn't. I find a hit but digging deeper
reveals a fatal flaw or maybe
i'm just looking too hard

i'm dropping down a step or notch
i had whisky but maybe scotch
would have been a better choice
give me that microphone
i've been sitting here all night
and you said it would be all right

an evening with the movie queens
and kings up on the hill
showed your pull and hold on
me and my needy little pawn
pushed around the board
bullies, blues, and thieves

crossing the line we lose a day
but gain our soul, in a crate that
fell from first class, a crate that
spells the death of our brother
brooklyn holds the charmer underneath

the green day is really sick and misery
flies from the board as they try
to bring forth on holiday

no pressure. no pressure. no pressure
this isn't good. we need pressure
this isn't good. kill the pressure

the dawning of the rest of our lives
this is the life on holiday
until it is found for what it is
and what it isn't. is. isn't

off to empty roads
to walk alone
i walk alone

my shadow is beating and fighting
i wish they would find me
my shadow is dancing the line
i wish they would find me
my shadow is the only thing that wakes inside me
i walk alone

their shadows want to walk inside me
they want to tramp all over my stuff. my stuff
if they tramp, they will die. i will make sure of that
if they tramp, they will cry. i will make sure of that
if they tramp, kill them before they cry
then make sure of it

a touch, a squirt, a repeat. no way of doing it
drop the shy act. work it hard. this is the sht

could disclaimers be any worse?
Line them all up and shoot them
right in the middle of a good dream, something burbbled
up, "I think I you love"
so what am I so afraid of?
A love there is not cure enough

this is just pop dribble. throws this crap out.
turn it down
too much loving going on. that makes much
i outsourced it. I OUTSOURCED IT!!!
it's a sweet joke. 2:30am is a sweet joke too
but a nasty one. znrumsn hsndhe dsyd ell

see the glory of the royal
the glory of the wonder or wonder how
i need wood lock. i can't see straight any more

the streak is running it off. I'll argue my case

near 3, fading
139 is a weak one
so is off
fade.tw.gky

losing it
how it is no now
done now

think about it

in a fit of circumspection
i lost my reflection
think about it
yeah, i'll think about it

walked away and came out
stronger than before
ended up in the same place
but with a different face

hope you like the new we
and wonder what you'll
think about it
and what i'll
think about it

four

push
edge
flow

push
know
pull

make
pain
real

heal
your
pain

give
many
take
some
tear
down

push
edge
flow

love
real
love

slipknow

why did you hang around this place?
did you get hooked on these plots
or maybe the drama of watching
me burn and twist of my own
devices and toy with the fire
in my eye and the pits that
slowly pull the light from
the skies and the high
that crashes without
a splash because
when it hits it
has no mass
or heaven
to pray
save
me

.

slip, know

used to play

i used to sing i was the omega man
always talking to myself
and i did too. walk down the street
mumbling to myself. afraid to touch
the gaze of another for fear that i might
find something in myself or in them. in them
that would be the worst. i used to play

i thought tokyo was bad. but that was just
a warmup act for a much bigger stage
baby, you should see me now. or maybe not
i'm not quite ready for my closeup

the hell you say. i agree. fanfare for this common man
but i'm far from common. ordinary. normal. sane.
take your pick
you can label me right now but by the time you speak
you'll miss a beat and i slip a measure
find the time. lose the rhyme. lose the beat. find the turn
around. a round life. a round ball. i used to play

she buried me in a print impossible
cyan running deep between my mind
but this other she took me and walked
raw haze swung left and missed

an opportunity to slide out and back in
hey baby, where are you coming from?
you stepped into my world and left yours in
a back room with a light swinging
and cases stacked like dreams
but stay out of both and find your own
a fine team. you'll pick first. i used to play

i've got the key to the highway but no gas
left in the tank and i'm a little short
can you spare some change? wait that's
been my fear for far too long. hang on. hold tight

layla came and whispered in my ear.
she hasn't done that
for many years but i thought i heard her say,
"please leave me alone."
so i'm back with white lightning and wine
and too many j's hurting me in different ways
i trusted them all, and took it hard thinking
it was all my fault. put down the pick. i used to play

break the glass in case you need a ragged edge to
compare where you've been to where you might
end up if you can't get a bit of sleep in a corner
of someone's life especially your own

own. funny word. don't really own it
only the way you feel about it and see about
getting a hand to pick up the pieces of the mirror
that worked so well but walked away because
she had to grow beyond the mercury smeared on the
smooth surface, perfect except for the line of tears
"you should get those removed," he said
no, no...it's perfect the way it is. i used to play

t minus

t minus 7 and counting
seems that's the way these days
actually since the far east sun
showed the walls so steep
and feelings running deep

or maybe it was before
we've been down this road
before but each time is more
easy and hard, yin and yang
micro bursts and big bang

ok, i don't get it, it'll be alright
ok, i don't sweat it
it'll be alright

always easier when you're out first
and can sit and watch from the side
but when it's gone offline the mind
loves to run and bake pies and cakes
sweet with the hurt i always make

ok, i don't like it, it'll be alright
ok, i can't take it
it'll be alright

i really ought to know by now
how i'll feel when it hits
doctor can you see me
again this week?

ok, i won't fight it, it'll be alright
ok, i can't right it
it'll be alright

t minus 6 and counting
beautiful fish run through your fingers
the hard land of the winter coming
make it more than it is this time
if the snapshot holds stay sublime

ok, i can't mold it, it'll be alright
ok, i can't hold it, it'll be alright

ok, i can take it, it'll be alright
ok, i can fake it, it'll be alright
ok, I can make it

post watts muse

dreaming dreams that seem to make
sense but then when she says to think
about it something kicks the gut and
sends me reeling, steeling a glance
hoping that she was kidding but
she wasn't

banking dark, bringing stark
reminders
of days and times left standing
in the rain soaked memory or is it
tears that kill the pain

after so many years of filling up
you have to dig out and empty
a life full of hardened edges made
blunt by constant teacher pounding
passed for love now you know that
she wasn't

banking dark, makers mark
remembers
feelings pushed back into boxes
flipping clocks and purple toxic
tears that leave a stain

step into the void step lightly
even though the hardest joy
is found in walking apart because
if you don't you'll never know if
you really felt and if you can't
she wasn't

banking dark , tiring park
re-injures
a weakened joint missed the point
and sailed past a chance for
tears that break the chain

third slice

early 2007

spark

banking dark
brings a spark
take a picture and leave your future
loving summer what will you do
feel like a person you can find
it's a long way to your mind

banking dark
praying spark
somebody inside never been done
wonderful tonight leaves a trace
breathing hard in the space
between the notes my love

banking dark
filling spark
one slip walks away from me

it isn't stopping

dear, kiss me once more
that i may wear your love
and be free from this ache
that isn't stopping

jesus walked on the water
turned the water into wine
we drink the wine and touch
our glasses, everything is fine

a number not in service
under cover of the night
spirits fly from the gorge
to santee leaving it all behind

lines of poetry sing a mystery
but its few and far between
a caring touch instead of
a harsh word overheard

there's a place named for my dad
and the home we never had
the only chance now is to work
and keep from passing it on

damaged

looking for shelter from the storm that
brews within licking a raw inside cut
a bad boy who's lost his way

a runner on the sands of war with a kit
full of sister morphine and bloody gauze
homecoming to the pipes that play

tossing fastballs warmed up too fast
but that was just an excuse to no try
and stay with the familiar sting

not ready when the first one came along
the vacuum scares him, that'll work
reading meters, checking out, never there

the second was a mistake but can't send it back
so settle in for the long haul in suit and tie
in by 7 out by 5 and gone the rest of the time

can't really blame you, never had a chance
too bad you had to take me down too
didn't have the tools to make it work

hurry sundown so we can leave this place
under cover of the night we're all the same
and he'll never find us here

damaged one and all but this still
makes me shake my head and wonder
and fight my way out of the enveloping haze

point

left point driving right
here i thought it might
feel ok or at least not sting
as bad as some of the other things

turns out it does and rather now
intensifies as i'm feeling how
i didn't before and clearly see
what a tidy mess lies before me

time to unpack and stay awhile
despite it feeling like being on trial
for crimes committed by the mother
and counsel now left for another

discerning folk will pass it by
another search can let you try
to live and learn and love to be
alone together, myself and me

trades

a clarion call foretells a bending palm
loose in the trades arching away from
the howl that stings your face in a place
of abject beauty overtaken by plastic and
aluminum yet still the trades get their way
tossing chaise into lagoons made by digging
not by the moon and the water

coupled up surrounds me but on this trip
it's only me and mini me although he is different
or maybe not instead a sign of what i seek
and am afraid to find amidst the trades

voices overheard from under the dome
hint of home left but soon rediscovered when
the bill comes due and the tram makes its
final stop at the lobby turning out the red
and raw and tired ready to tell the tales and
show the pictures of fun and sun now done
not really knowing what was taken by the trades

strike three

you don't get four strikes?
who made that rule?
they guy with the bit of drool
running down his chin?

the towers are turning
the ties are burning
the seas are churning
and a rock is tossed into the water

my sister pulled me aside
then cheated as i rolled
over and entered a private hell
and lie in a sagging farewell
waiting for hell to pay
and my brother to say
that it was all a bad dream

keep it down in there
too much noise how can i
sleep you accident that ruined
my nice little solo gig

gray skies and brown leaves
tennis shoes and short sleeves
means i'm not going to stay
not really up for a passion play

pulling the love out after
the year of tears and laughter
alone it seems rubbing my eyes
unable to hide despite my disguise

doctor can you see my fire
the wind that doesn't require
the earth to hold for so long
going down left is oh so wrong

strike three writing back
sorry son but mostly you never hear
destined to wander not able to steer
no response station we're out
strike three writing black

get your coat

wind is pushing the palms
time is crushing the calm
a wry smile garners no doubt
little left to gather or shout
about as it slides on down

i can see very well
where this all might sell

stuck...more later

park canto

she would hint but wouldn't say
if it's too late for me to see

Grace at play, dancing, dreaming, singing
a song with verses I never wrote
a melody swinging without my touch
a beat that was never shared
and when i asked instead she
sat with it and kept it tight
instead, said, "think about it"

the ink flows and reminds me
black smears on the paper hint at
the mess left behind, unpaid bills
red letter days, changing ways
whispers of vespers, do you really
have to go that far, i guess it wasn't
nearly enough to anchor the rope or
pull hard enough and fast enough
to take up the slack or realize that
you needed to cast off the lines

a rising tide will carry you and spare you the pain
instead joy shining like the pearl you are
luminous, blinding, the light and the heat
healing deep wounds, salve for those you touch
and yourself
your self
beautiful self

standing still

why is it that when this song comes on
everything stands still
it all fades from view
pastels and charcoal lines
trailing off into the ether
raising ire or confusion in the spectators
how do you explain time and matter standing still?
gluons and muons pausing in respect
for something even more fundamental
hit the left arrow, I need pause again
profoundly tragic, defying logic, misty magic

standing still seeming static
stillness lies about the the island
underneath a dreamer, a schemer
taking a knife in the back despite the best
intentions, dr. klyser writes a new test
please check your weapons at the couch

differing opinions on whether to pick up
or put down the phone
curbing expectations, excoriations, and parade floats
glued on flowers and seed of discontent
the viewing area just screws up traffic
forgive me if I get just a bit graphic
but at some point you just call it a day no matter
how he shaped the clay before it was fired
sent to the cabinet because he didn't have the tools

weak signals growing stronger, hurting longer
stringing along the knots you can't untie
so you just cut the string and throw the mess out
a waste? denying your caste? decide in haste?
i suppose i could sit and untangle the mess
and try to fix family fortunes field
standing still singing static

this will be

this will be
whatever flies free
from an open heart
and a damp face

this will be
whoever can see
the real me inside
take a peek

open quickly with pressed slacks
and squeaking shoes tied
too tight but maybe too much
up front as wednesday
will never come

this will be
wherever we flee
sent reeling by words
sitting is hard

this will be
however i'll see
it through to the end
to the other side

wednesday

a two day window, a lucky strike
the second was the one that stuck
and plucked from the stack
dictating reams and filling in
a backstory that can't win

see the lights from the city
knowing it might fall to pity
heart beating like a bass drum
but wednesday will never come

fogbound and grounded
strictly on instruments for now
couldn't stand the weather
turn around and go back home
not the first to roam

driving the hills the slow turns
may be gone but the fire still burns
my heart feeling a little numb
but wednesday will never come

fourth slice

early 2007

all back

yell now, stomp your feet
the trees are bending
an offering, a message
to take it all in, receive it
and give it all back

sun breaking through
mist falls away
i've quit screaming
and tilting at windmills
turn around give it back

shrubs in fine rows
doors that never really close
in my mind strike a pose

boplicity reigns supreme
a love so true
green in blue
pounding on the skin
no double reed this time

walk calm but firm
release the grip
hold on gently
bare feet on the coals
but nothing burns

lines crossing the marsh
birds taking easy flight
leaving all that is harsh

betray

he sold me out
i was just looking
for a place to rest
go back inside
although i'm tired of staying
in slanting shadows and gazing
longingly at those turned inside out

he sold me out
i didn't ask for much
just that he hold his tongue
cover my ears
pretend not to hear
but he spread it like manure
acrid and sticky in the heat

he sold me out
tried to let it go
but it comes back in a dream
barbed at the tip
special knots that make
mobius green with envy
and setting aside the black

demon down

arise! awake! but be still
and feel the lonely beat
lub dub lub dub
counting on the out
and trying not to crawl
out of your own skin

hear a step
open an eye
take a breath
stare the demon down

burning both sides
of a wax philosophic
drip drip drip
stinging puddles fly
and harden hearts
with silly sayings

see the past
feel the present
give the future
take the demon down

countdown barking loud
buzzing with excitement
tick tock

now's the time
hit the high c
and leave it be

sound the alarm
turn that down
cut me up
run the demon down

wish i could dance

only love can set you free
i was wrong when i wrote that song
twenty some odd years ago
it seems like five lifetimes
since i walked in the rain
and felt it running down my face
i wish i could dance

on patrol in the desert
i got the letter and saw the tape
made it all so very clear
but still held out hope
having to dig in and dig out
a few months pass by
i wish i could dance

rounding out the shattered nights
blocking out the neon lights
and sounds of the city pounding
my head like a heavy bag
stood there and took it
dished out all by myself
i wish i could dance

they don't come around much
although a change was in the wind
sorry i couldn't say more
but i'm tattered and torn
had finally edged forward
and slipped before i fell
i wish i could dance

nothing

a little stick, it doesn't sting
but makes you wonder
and take the referral
closing from both sides
probably nothing
don't think it's anything
probably nothing

spin at six, turn at seven
shouldn't have ate
that first or second course
supposed to be low
probably nothing
not really anything
probably nothing

ask the question
believe the answer
take the test
and hope you pass
probably nothing
don't think anything
probably nothing

fades

it goes apart and comes around
rises up and settles down
waiting for the second stays
feeling like the winsome fades

message post in the night
away from the masses sight
at some point comment stops
from black to white it fades

characters of the mother tongue
slash and cross a lonely one
with no translation just assume
distance grows and reeling fades

seeking help from an old script
years have passed, the record skipped
stuck in a groove and scratching ties
and slowly dies the music fades

streak

streaking symbols shine and sparkle
it hurts to look
dance and flit turning orange
in the dropping distance
sputtered filaments not yet glowing
too early for this one

head to tail, red to black
fish soaring in spite of
or because of
no, wait, and...and

trails through the marsh
were adventure some time back
now seem small and painful
but only because the eyes
are tired and the heart
is mired
currying favor
misplaced glory
same old story
dressed up goodbye
from both that came before
and now silent
stinging quiet
void

it hurts to look but still i do
the shimmer beckons
siren song looking for a cove
to gather up and strike back
burst forth
turning
twisting
releasing
fall

happy snippet

if 5 was 7
it could be better
feeling suicidal
praying for revival
on the cold yellow tile
and a hot stream tries
to rinse off the edge

hanging head trying
to catch a breath in between
drops falling mixed with
everything else that came
before and after
never during

but duty calls
no time to rest
seems so long ago
can't even remember
what rest is
was
could be
upcoming test
maybe absent
just can't climb
sometimes no
is all i can do

absolutely

the prose flows from her
in beautiful arcs
brightly sprinkled voicing
that captivates and inspires
absolutely

an old soul but young
at heart and wise beyond
her tears that nourish art
so stunning she cannot yet see
absolutely

shining star streaking far
beyond what those around her
can see or feel or dream
beautiful dancer pirouettes
absolutely

deepest lover sheds the covers
armored no more instead
walks until the clack
then sits and breathes
absolutely

letting go and knowing that
every moment is a fresh start
she feels it all and braves it all
a precious soul that embodies grace
absolutely

fifth slice

mid 2007

day make

what a difference a day
make it count make it wear
and tear and stare off
into a distant past passed on

rain reversing direction
falling up, failing up
flailing up and wiggle
second, third, fourth
chance to start but really
just quit counting

not caring, not knowing
but showing signs of time
actually spent not dreaming
shrinking away from dark
praying for the light
end to the night
end to more
or less

pound off

quintero allure was walking
no, running, really
away or from, doesn't really matter
far too mercurial, a mad hatter
squelching rumors and clandestine pies
binds that tie, kissing lies
a moot cycle indeed

the road to abbey was new
laid down in a trough
and gutter snipes laughing
but not enough staffing
to make a difference
a real difference
not a sears difference

the clams smell great
shuck one, pearl two
but aching muscles require
a helping hand, lost the band
a love that's canned
and stored for a rainy day
expiration notwithstanding

i miss

i miss the laugh of the boy
i miss his youth that is running away
blink and you miss it
pray that you don't
that you can stay in the moment
and view the world through his eyes

i miss dropping in and ducking
i miss the washing machine
nature having her way
and me letting her
wet quiet in a swirling storm

i miss my strings to pluck
i miss my string to stab
joining in the chorus
chasing the groove
touching what has no form

i miss myself sometimes
i miss who i could be
caught up in sorrows
chasing tomorrows
instead of just being to be

i miss you
i miss me
i miss the look
i miss the eyes
i miss the look

long time down

a california classic, or so i thought
a fanciful breed that couldn't be bought
or sold out my second-hand soul
sorting things that have taken a toll

it's a long time down
come back into town
it's a long time down

sitting pretty, silly little ditty
living on a couch with no pity
losing my edge and slowly settle
remember the feel of the twisting metal

it's a long time down
still won't quite bend
it's a long time down

to be continued...

cry a little

fall or falter, doesn't matter
which you say it still feels like
i need to cry a little because
each day i die a little but not
how you'd really expect

a character, a sweeping arc
crossed lines and radicals
flexing feet to drain the twist
and fighting the red mist
of what i couldn't get past

i wished, i tried, i sighed
and settled down into a lull
slung chair moving pillows
it isn't soft, just in the way
used to be thrilling, but now
just tiring, sad, and running

but you can't run
i follow you
you can't split
unless you're ready
for four pieces
six in the room
and two alone

chasing

looking down
and hoping
to see it
to feel it
chasing
but it's
never
the same
or sane
chasing
it passed
the past
is gone
i see it
languid
bittersweet
chasing

mindful

mindful mopping never stopping
to feel the wet as i squeeze it out
of tendrils gray and ragged then
dump what's left in the street

meta five, as four is not enough
to explain how far i've come but
never alone and still not as the
look remains elusive still with
only one or maybe two before

quintano came back again just
to say hi and thumb his nose
at what i thought i left behind

but the fronds are being tossed
by waves i can't see and the two
are rather lost, or rather left me
behind in a fine dust, crushed
quartzsite and dreams spilling
through the narrow opening

quintano mocks me now
laughing at my inability
to look past thinly

cranes erecting or dredging
to build or clean and leverage
a rusting shell left out for
too many seasons

quintano just shakes
frozen ropes
at his feet

sixth slice

mid 2007

dimming

why is that light so bright?
trying to show my feelings
no, i don't mind, although
it hurts and I'm losing track
just falling through the cracks

just take me home because
i don't remember why i left
feeling kind of sick
please take me home

what will it be tonight?
keep smiling through
a little bit of insanity rains
down from the heavens
we'll meet again
some sunny day

zero for two

is it zero for two
and two for naught?
i hope not
maybe later
radio silence

i remember a fire pot
and burning pictures
and letters
but she was 19
and i watched

up in flames
no wonder
i felt the burn
eating away
ashes blowing
scattered

outperform

outperformed redress sinking sadly
into a sea of acetic dreams but none
taken back into the night

the race is on, full mass
from the back of the grid
stood up just to fall back down
rough up the surface so maybe
this coat will stick for awhile

ruling my world would be divine
if only i could find what's mine
instead of filling up the day
tended to by the white suits
lollipops and sours sticking
to the floor. i can't talk

killing me softly with words
and no words, not a peep
tourmaline turned down
great lengths wasted
favors seldom tasted
then frozen. i can't run

a flat world, around she goes
where it stops god knows
but i can't tell as i'm sliding
down the concrete supporting
god knows what, door is shut
and locked. i can't walk

within one hour

why look now?
is it curiosity or
languid punishment
just close it down
put away the thorns
within one hour

active or hidden
doesn't really matter
when the call comes
if it comes and you
actually can answer
within one hour

from a perilous tip
two different sightings
and clearing the air
or so you thought
pushing a little hard
within one hour

what

what am i doing?
where am i going?
this isn't a dress rehearsal
if we have to spend the semester figuring
then we won't get much work done

a thousand words to say a hundred things
about ten feelings in one person
what is going on here?

was it planned this way?
who's responsible?

ok, let me start again
fresh start
let me take this from the top
those paintings scare me

x-ray and shades
lower body cracks
bent over no casting

i want faders not knobs
push instead of twiddle
roam instead of fiddle
as if only

timing

out of phase was
the first time out
the one that saved me
restored my faith
in love and touch

but no matter how sweet
searing gentle passion
physics is physics
waves can construct
or subtract
or just flatten
timing is everything

a battle of primal urges
vs. bad experiences
takes a toll over time
even if it comes full circle
the center has moved
and can't reconnect
timing is everything

perspective is relative
picasso turned the corner
when one is on the down
and the other is in it thick
light can play tricks
dancing dark apart
timing is everything

framed

framed by black squares
gentle touch, fiery eyes
pillows falling without
sound or fury but
prescient passion

smiling deeply
seeing through it
pass the past
make it last
beyond the moment

still uncertain
but feeling it edge
towards the one
who sees the beauty
and says so

jade heart

a jade heart cradled
in twisted mesh
green blades reaching
squared blocks seeking
meaning held by brass
it sits surrounded
but open to something new

a jade heart hidden
drilled steel tubing
purple flowers blooming
shine the light
shine all day
pull in the slack
but cast off the lines

a jade heart beating
a gaping hole shrinking
pain pushed to the back
seeking release and healing
touched by daring
pausing for the rhythm
to catch up

a jade heart joining
the rest of the strands
trailing from the frame
worlds tucked into foam
crawling towards a place
that is new and warm
away from pine and pain
the stains left behind

a jade heart moving
into the light
reflecting angles
the quantum view
new connections
leaving equations
unsolved
but tended

seventh slice

late 2007

mercy wheels

no point in direction
it's coming no matter what
say goodnight sweet prince
your fight was gallant
your methods flawed
your heart tragic
don't be afraid to cry
before you know it will pass
everyone will remember you
until they drop the rose and walk past

mercy is trying to visit
but the barricades are strong
dreams made of heat in your heart
waiting for darkness to come
and steel quickly
wishing for arms to hold
passing it off as fancy
but desperate
for tenderness
and mercy

you had a good run
and thought that living was
running to keep up
and keep tabs

may grace be with you
because mercy is scarce
but i fear you'll feel neither
you were taught to win
but never learned to fail
pick it up on the fly
or during the fall
find a way home

mercy dear mary
slaughtered before waking
closing doors and bolting ways
swinging remains reminding
of lives that spun out
pirouette and pratfall
packing boxes
cleaned out after you're gone

living in seven time
but it's an eightfold world
you tap your feet
but mercy doesn't feel the beat
the end of the sky
shivering hues and streaks
you loved the texture
until you could really feel it
now it's too much

mercy come
the mourners are singing
mercy save
your broken soul
mercy love
your analog pulse
before it is quiet

dragged by your feet
to do it again
until it's really wrong
you're on your knees
mercy wheels
turning again

breakdown

waiting for a breakdown
around the corner
clock watching
twisted dove
sweet relief
barely there

leg fidget
body widgets
falling down
tearing mildew
hope it cleans
inside out

curl up tight
the way out
many loose ends
can't let down
won't stay up
help from joe
waiting for a breakdown

climbing

climbing hills
standing still
or at least it
felt that way
butt kicked
treats no trick
called out but
stuck in there
lingered then left
no heart theft
patience

windows

window of opportunity
open or closed
ragged confusion
sometimes you miss it
leave a wake rebuffed
sad and lonely sorting
tripping the light
of the things unsaid
turnaround takes time
miss a beat
coming in late
wondering

so sweet

the missing link broken
her lies were so sweet
but what do you need
when your turn is beat
and the news has gone to seed

slide that socket over
strings so silky and jones
would sing into the night
cold feeling in my bones
dancing alone was such a sight

i seem to get what i need
despite my best intentions
no matter what i do or say
waves crashing surly inventions
dear, do you mind if i stay?

three octobers

it's not about me
or about you either
don't look too deep
or read between
the lines in my face
they leave no trace
just feeling the space
around three octobers

tired of hearing jive
shucking empty oysters
or holding court
raise your left hand
and pledge undying
love without crying
the mirror isn't lying
about three octobers

is this the one that
sticks and leaves no
stone unturned and
shines a light on all
the darkest corners
touching the mourners
joining beautiful foreigners
between three octobers

tyger

tyger burning bright
such a sight
quickly twitching feet
losing my seat
but maybe it's time
to stand

time and distance
such resistance
to move along and see
what would be
if i just let things
play against the sky

sometimes swinging tides
lick the salt from the rim
a cadillac ranch and dance
dipping deep across the floor

tyger burning tight
made the flight
boarding pass in peril
lined up where all
kids break down
and cry

back to open arms
bet the farm
but venture slowly
beloved lowly
things to see
places to be

while seated

while seated
please fasten hope
to my poor ailing legs
i'll drag it as best i can
i'll try to be the real man
just don't make me beg
sliding down a slope
while seated
i can't run fast
i barely know the way
thought there was a map
i tried to bridge that gap
ran out of things to say
know it can't last
while seated
i'm not flying this
but i can see outside
hazy grid laid out looking
a drunken spider cooking
snacks for a long ride
into the abyss
while seated

eighth slice

2008

sifting

dark clouds lifting, slowly sifting
through yesterday's fog of war
battle-worn and breaking the chains
slipping away, letting go, finding more

self fulfilling just stop instilling
there isn't always something wrong
rising tides will catch the morning light
unless you keep playing that damn song

pinched quandary

pinched quandary for sailors
frozen peas or corn
for the cellulose
swelling down
abrupt

listen closely so you don't miss
a single thing
carefully sighting the possible
the permissible
free reign providing you cover
all the costs

whistling hand grenades
past a willing few
east st. louis
toodle de doo
it's jazz, dammit
swing it or else

shot in the foot
i can't believe i
shot him in the foot
how could i?
breathe, settle, squeeze
don't pull down on me
instead i need traction

the deep end

i'm feeling a little peaked
maybe it's just the heat
i'm passing those defeated
at least it tastes like meat

i'm chewing up my fine time
dropping leaflets on the news
i'm reading all the fine print
and you're covered if i lose

stay away from the deep end
i know you love it so
stay away from the deep end
i know yours likes to grow

i'm much bigger than the sea
but oceans apart from being
i'm smaller casting shadows
but still having trouble seeing

we're combining things except
that stupid fold-out couch
we're dividing things, respect
how my boxes seem to slouch

i'm seeing the deep end
as a last resort and refuge
i'm bleeding in the deep end
dry within the deluge

i'm out of the deep end
i shouldn't have to defend
every third word
and maybe a fourth
bring me a fifth
tell me, chi le ma?

i laugh at the deep end
but feel left out
like the serious ones passed me
without even asking
going to save someone else
or themselves

a deepening scar doesn't stretch
its tight but holds in place
the angle of omission
the memory and the pace

i'm plugging in my cables
my signal is now quite strong
i'm turning up my faders
'gonna drown out his stupid song

rice recovered and now in the molds
i'll use the potatoes and capture the role
of the white cotton and blue frog buttons
flying north might help to make it whole

i'm draining the deep end
so we can skate the curves cleanly
i'm draining the deep end
where the water's best sent begging
i'm filling the shallow end
this is over

i'm stepping through your window
trying hard to avoid the pane
i'm looking for a clean t-shirt
'cause this one's wet from the rain

i'm afraid of the deep end
i'm just too tired to swim
i'm afraid of the deep end
i can't live up to him

oh, great, now he's here
not like it couldn't get much worse
he's diving in. he's the swan
the water knows he's coming
they bead and sweat away
it's time, the swan is coming

lead him towards the deep end
we'll get him after dinner
violent redirection and repulsion
does wonders if you're thinner

the swan thinks it is won, but those
are shallow end rules
in the deep end it changes
and all bets are off
except the one between me and you
i'll double down there and give you odds

nothing sucks me in
now i'm routed out
integral lost in translation
the derivatives will shout

i'm rolling my eyes but can't help it
like to stand up and make amends
i'm still going to ruin your time here
and stay clear of your deep ends

stonking complex

warbirds in flight, bringing the fight
down to the ground the dirty ground
make a hole, play a role, dirty ground
spinning on 5 axes, see the vm now

happy peach with the right chicken
counting off one-two one-three
but 4 is death, don't say it loud
no reason to be proud propped up

that stonking complex is meta fast
but slowly losing grip on the last tip
that he got, then forgot, then walked
around a may pole hiding as an antenna

signal. he had no signal. I want a signal
I just need some help, time to yelp

pearls before me

why yes, i'd love to see
the washington monument
but not get dropped on top
and slide on down
unable to stop

be careful to toss
your pearls before me
i'd love to have tea
but don't think i'm up
for a trip under the sea

the view must be fabulous
you can see everything
the lookouts will sing
like the trees but be careful
the bees tend to sting

i waited to cross
the pearls before me
only wanted to be
a bit player rather than
the star that you see

looking back i fought the draft
and marched in the streets
i was feeling complete
but mother had other
ideas for me to meet

the day the music died wasn't
nearly as sad as this dog
lost in a thick fog
wishing that truck didn't
have so many apples
i wanted a pear
or maybe a peach

they all wasted
their pearls before me
enlightened and free
i cough and lightly sigh
before entering a plea

elevated musing

sitting in a blue flaky tube
wondering if the peels are talking
about something i should know about

a dirty mercenary sings
while Luke mugs on screen
listening to the conversation
canceling noise and meaning
i'm clear in my mind
steering my kindness

wishing for stinging obsession
naked and alive in my bed
a toe dipping into my head
needing a second pair of shades
pushing back the innocence lost

faults in all and seething still
that familiar ache wearing thin
unable to feel the skin
trying to hard to touch
the singing obsession
lit by candles

i'm keeping it to myself
Luke still struggles with two
a suburban dream
stigmata aside
my patience on needles and pins

spinning around to catch a glimpse
of that sad parade of players
serenading an empty table
the tenor stumbles
endless summer going down
fires burning hazy streaks
into a lazy sideways

my darling daydream
harmonics hanging like

notes sliding just below
perfect pitch
nobody cares

i don't hear him any more
letting my battles slide
watching Luke try to touch
a blue wall
whatever, amen

keep on talking
hearing the party late
burning up midnight oil
sagging mattress swallows
a sitting duck
how many nights can
you go without sleep?

fumbling around and rolling over
and cover with the little blonde around the corner
swinging for the fences
but the director can't save
the second act
an original sin

he's taking pictures
i'm seeing my reflection
neither are pretty
stay away from the sauna
it'll leave you less
that you started with

never outside this state of confusion
can't remember who gets the bill
living five minutes at a time
means the clock does a lot of work

steering clear of the dusted neighbors
we brew our own concoctions
beautiful plumes
drawing back
making sure it's red
before you push it down

a hazy couch is sweet relief
i've seen that iron pot before
a little water in the bottom
to keep from sticking

back to the obsession thing
no way to sustain
and why does misery connect
pop, smoke, stay down
i've been hit

a window seat
in an aisle world
the system of the doctor
a frequent flier hell
just what you need
to make you feel better

looking outside
trying to change the weather
increase the temperature
to a balmy 42
wind at my tail
see your pink disk
show down the slowdown

quick cuts trickle down fast
stabbing glass and gamma rays
burn a hole in the collective
fueling my sleeper cell

where do we go from here
where do i go from here
i don't want to hear that song again
and long for the obsession
just because i said it
doesn't make it right
getting up in the middle on the night
watching the round and round
for the fiftieth time

heading north like a fragrant bird
bouncing lively and stiffening
to another southern breeze
twang and then it's gone
roll off the tele

saint theresa once sang about florida
or some such nonsense
i lost track of who's on the corner
making money and full of trash
bold as the hollow lights
higher than the king
higher than jesus
makes you feel like it at least

nobody ever saw you the way i do
or maybe i just missed the signs
clouded by a sour act of contrition
and double crossed at the junction

helical twist

a brown stocking cap pulled down
a strong gray rain failing down
never enough time to bring a dream
gently to a safe harbor

i'm sensing a storm that has been brewing
from a slow drip to a steady stream
infused with a helical twist
i'm seeing both sides now

he's certainly no stranger to pain
if only there was another place to put it
instead it seeps out in a broadcast
trying to stay clear of interference

i always wished i could realize
that indelible image that exists inside
and show him a graceful way
to move through this fractured life

expectations from a blackboard
falling down with a heady pace
in another time I'd climb that hill
and unlock that gold glass door

coroner's inquest

do you think i can float
i look good in this black coat

hanging around and just hanging on
video village goes silent
streaking the pink and the blue
and a goatee that comes and goes

just a question if you can float
dust off that long black coat
smoke hangs low for your test
closing the coroner's inquest

when did that chance pass by
to make it all right
instead I sit and craft
random cuts of nonsense

do you think you will float
I look good in a black coat

postscript

As with all slices, there are pieces remaining
on either side. But those are for another time
and place and slice.

For the ongoing saga:

nostatic.com/blog/

www.ingramcontent.com/pod-product-compliance
Lightning Source LLC
LaVergne TN
LVHW091314080426
835510LV00007B/487